A HISTORY OF AMLWCH

Iolo Wyn Griffiths

Text and photography copyright © 2016 Iolo Wyn Griffiths
All Rights Reserved

About the Author

Iolo is a Community Content Curator with a group of news in North Wales, and is keenly interested in genealogy and the local history of North Wales. His other publications include A History of Beaumaris (published in 2004), and two e-books, A History of Beaumaris, and A History of Bangor, which are available for Kindle via Amazon. The History of Bangor is also available on CreateSpace for print on demand. This History of Amlwch, and a History of Holyhead, by the same author, will both come out in Summer 2016, for both Kindle and CreateSpace.

Table of Contents

EARLY AMLWCH
THE PARYS MOUNTAIN COPPER MINES
THE GROWTH OF AMLWCH
AMLWCH PORT
SHIPBUILDING
OTHER INDUSTRIES
OIL
POSTAL SERVICES
EDUCATION
AMLWCH FREE SCHOOL
CHARITY SCHOOL
CIRCULATING SCHOOLS
NATIONAL SCHOOL
BRITISH SCHOOL
PRIVATE SCHOOLS
RHOSYBOL BRITISH SCHOOL
COUNTY SCHOOL
RELIGION
RHOSYBOL CALVINISTIC METHODIST CHURCH
HEALTH CARE
EISTEDDFODAU
AMLWCH AUTHORS
THOMAS JONES, TRANSLATOR
REV WILLIAM ROBERTS
OTHER AUTHORS
THOMAS COWBURNE (1737?-1815), PRINTER
WILLIAM ROOS, ARTIST (1808-73
LOCAL CHARACTERS
CADI RONDOL
BULL BAY
PORTH WEN BRICK WORKS
LLANEILIAN
USEFUL WEBSITES

EARLY AMLWCH

In the 14th century Amloch, as it was then called, was described as the town of the lakes, and the present town is built on the site of one of these lakes, after it was drained for industrial purposes. Today the area still retains many of these lakes, which attract a wide variety of birds.

In the 1352 Extent of Anglesey there is mention of a mill called Melin Isaf in the hamlet of Amlwch. Other hamlets mentioned in the parish in 1352 were Glasgraig, Bodsarthro, Bodgadfedd, Llechog, Trysglwyn and Bodhunod. Nearby Llaneilian had the hamlet of Bodgynddelw.

The existence of a farm called Bodednyfed could tempt one to assume a connection with Ednyfed Fychan, the ancestor of the Tudors. The truth is that this name is the map version of a name pronounced locally as Bodnyfa, and is the medieval township of Bodnyfaidd, home of a man called Nyfaidd, so any connection with Ednyfed Fychan, or any other Ednyfed for that matter, is based on a false etymology, derived from a misleading name on the map.

Before the discovery of the copper Amlwch was merely a hamlet, and a deep water creek where fishing boats could shelter during a storm, became a largish town, at one time the third largest in Wales.

Its lack of any importance just before the discovery of copper on Parys Mountain is clearly summed up in the 1760s by Lewis Morris, who described it as "No more than a cove between two steep rocks, a place of refuge provided the mouth of the rock can be discovered, which is now difficult for a stranger, and which had some trade in corn, butter and cheese.

THE PARYS MOUNTAIN COPPER MINES

Although discoveries locally of copper ingots with Roman inscriptions indicate that the Romans had mined on Parys Mountain, and some surface debris have been dated to nearly 4,000 years ago, to the Bronze Age, the modern large-scale mining only started in the 1760s.

An earlier modern enterprise was a great mineral work in Anglesey run by a Mr Medley in 1579, which produced a mineral water which made alum and copper. The details given by John Wynn of Gwydir leaves little doubt that this was on Parys Mountain. Unfortunately this venture was unprofitable and was abandoned, though the soil continued to be described throughout the 17th century as having a soil which produced copper and alum, with a survey of Anglesey by John Speed mentioning that alum and copperas was made there in his day, but the enterprise had been abandoned "without further hope because at first they saw it not answer their over-hastie expectations".

There are many candidates for the honour of having discovered the great mineral wealth on Parys mountain. In 1761 the Archdeacon of Merioneth's steward's horse stumbled on some old mineral workings (perhaps Medley's).

In 1762 a Scotsman called Alexander Fraser discovered another rich vein of minerals. Tradition asserts that he had fled for refuge to Wales after having killed a piper. He visited Parys Mountain, and then called on Sir Nicholas Bayly of Plas Newydd, and gave a flattering account of the prospect, and induced him to sink a shaft. Although ore was discovered, the mines flooded before any substantial quantity could be gotten, and the enterprise had to be abandoned.

The naval demand for copper for sheathing British warships created a market for high quality copper, and there was a demand for copper and brass objects for peaceful purposes, so there was great incentive to recommence mining operations. Copper sheathing protected warships from the growth of barnacles and seaweed, and also prevented boring by worms.

In 1764 a partnership from Macclesfield called Roe and Co was created to exploit the already existing Penrhyn Du copper mines at Llanengan near Pwllheli, and a condition of their lease of that mine from Sir Nicholas Bayly was that they should also mine the Parys Mountain which was regarded as something of a white elephant. Although ore was discovered, the cost of digging it far outweighed the profits, and at length they considered abandoning the works.

The Penrhyn Du agent, Jonathan Roose, was sent to Parys Mountain with orders to close the mine, but as a last attempt, he allowed his men to sink shafts in various places 800 yards of a place he called the Golden Venture. He suspected that a cupreous spring he discovered must have come from a rich body of mineral, and the date generally given for the discovery of the rich body of ore and hence the Parys Mountain copper boom is March 2, 1768, and the man widely credited with starting the copper boom was Rowland Pugh, who took on the bargain which contained a good vein of ore.

Rowland Pugh was rewarded for his discovery with a bottle of brandy, the honour of chairing at the anniversary of the discovery, but also the more worthwhile reward of a cottage rent-free for the rest of his life.

Soon afterwards Edward Hughes of Llys Dulas, who owned the eastern part of Parys Mountain, started another venture, the Parys Mine Company in 1778, along with John Dawes, the banker who financed his enterprise, and the lawyer Thomas Williams (later nicknamed Twm Chwarae Teg, because of his fair dealings with the workers).

Meanwhile, the Roe and Company lease of the other part of the mountain expired, and the Earl of Uxbridge, later Marquess of Anglesey, took over these mines.

The success of the enterprises led to the two major landowners, the Earl of Uxbridge and the Rev Edward Hughes having two elegant houses built in Amlwch for their occasional residence, namely Mona Lodge and Parys Lodge.

Illustration 1: Mona Lodge (Public domain)

During the height of modern mining operations, as many as 2,000 men, women and children were engaged in digging and processing the ore. At that time Parys Mountain produced 80,000 tonnes of ore each year (said to exceed the entire production of Cornwall) was regarded as the greatest copper mine in the world. Women and children were given the relatively light task of breaking up the ores with hammers.

An observer in the 19th century described the copper ladies as skilled and able women who were held in great respect by the miners. As well as being hard-working, they were praised for keeping their homes in good order, and a popular song of the time even suggested that they did not receive enough for what they did.

The employment of women at the mines followed the fortunes of the mines. In the 1851 census, 65 women were listed as copper miners, but by 1881 this number had declined to 14, and by 1891 had declined further to only one.

The mining was largely open cast, with the mountain stripped of its herbage, and perforated with numerous caverns, and the workers being lowered on wooden platforms to the workface. When W Bingley visited the mine in 1798, the ore was roasted in kilns, and the sulphureous smell made it seem to him "like the vestibule to Tartarus."

Other visitors to Amlwch who took an interest in the copper mining ctivities included James Watt, who patented improvements to the steam engine, which had been invented by Newcomen, and the scientist Michael Faraday.

Having such a lot of workers in a district with no banks and a shortage of small change, meant that extraordinary measures were needed to pay the wages. Some of the copper was used to make the famous Parys Mountain penny tokens in 1787, followed by halfpenny tokens. These tokens with the Anglesey Mines Company monogram on one side and a Druid's head on the other, also had the unusual attraction of containing a copper content equal to their face value. They were well received by the public and were accepted widely. They were superior to the king's official coinage. Tokens were declared illegal in 1797, after the king had commissioned Matthew Boulton of Birmingham to produce official copper coinage.

The tokens are dated between1787 and 1793, and over 200 varieties were made, with different number of acorns in the wreath, type styles, and difference in the smile on the druid's face.

Two men stand out in the industrial history of Amlwch, namely Thomas Williams and James Treweek.

Thomas Williams (1737-1802) was an Anglesey lawyer who became one of the most important figures of the Industrial Revolution in Britain. His connection with Amlwch began when he was called in by the Lewis family of Llys Dulas to sort out their boundary claim to part of Parys Mountain when copper was discovered there. He became involved in the business and joined with two others to create the Parys Mine Company which was eventually to employ 800 workers. He then formed a second, the Mona Mine Company, which gave him control of mining the other side of the mountain.

These two companies were to become one of the greatest industrial projects of the 18th century and made Thomas Williams a wealthy man. He built smelting works at Amlwch, Ravenhead and Swansea and brass and copper works at Holywell, in South Wales and the Thames Valley; there were offices and stores in Liverpool and he diversified with commercial ventures in Chester, Bangor and Caernarfon. He also took over the Cornish copper industry. By 1800 it was claimed that half the copper market was in the hands of Thomas Williams.

He was quick to contribute to the new church in Amlwch in 1800, and farmed his lands wisely.

The copper industry was so successful that Thomas Williams, a one-time country solicitor (nicknamed Twm Chwarae Teg, because of his fairness in his dealings), issued a token coinage of copper halfpennies and pennies which was readily accepted in Chester and Liverpool. The Parys Mountain coinage, with the design of a Druid's head, had a high copper content.

Treweek's association with Amlwch came through the Cornish copper industry. He came to Amlwch from Cornwall in 1811, as manager of the new Mona Mine Company. He left Cornwall when the mines there faced a hard time, and worked at Swansea for a while where he worked for the Vivian family.

His responsibilities as the manager of the Mona Mine Company were varied. He superintended all the mining operations and had a staff of several hundred. He organised transport of goods to and from the mine, using local farmers with their carts. He had the power to grant or refuse work, never a popular situation for a manager. He fixed rates of pay for piece work, dealt with strikes, and saw to medical services at the mine, where accidents were frequent.

In 1826 he was put in charge of the Company, sinking mines, at the Mona Works, and in 1828 he was made manager of the Parys Works, and in 1828 he was also made overseer of the Copper Smelting Works.

After 1833, until his death in 1851 he was in charge of everything connected with copper mining and the Amlwch copper trade, and was manager of the two Amlwch companies. It is thanks to his ability in all these fields that the copper industry in Amlwch flourished as it did.

By the 1830s the quality of the ore mined started to deteriorate, mirroring the decline of British and European mines, while North American mines with superior yields were developing rapidly. British ores rarely yielded more than 8%metal, while Cuban ores yielded 27% copper, and Australian ores could yield 40%.

Illustration 2: An early engraving of mining on Parys Mountain (Public domain)

Even expensive new equipment and new management failed to halt this decline, and after 1833 there were no references to the Anglesey mines in the Mining Reports in the North Wales Chronicle.

The price of copper later fell due to cheaper foreign ores, and the remaining ore reserves on Parys Mountain were less accessible, so the copper industry declined, so by 1904 the mines closed, and a guidebook for Anglesey said that "the great mines are deserted, and that Amlwch is fast becoming the resort of persons desirous of passing restful days in the midst of natural beauty." Pictures from that period would illustrate the dereliction which has by the overtaken the small harbour.

Illustration 3: The lunar landscape of Parys Mountain, with the remains of the old windmill which was used for draining the mineshafts

Remains of the machinery can still be found on the mountain, in a fragile condition, including the tower of the old engine house, which supplied the power to operate the many ropeways, and a windmill built in 1878 to assist in pumping water out of the mines. Initially this was to prevent flooding, so that miners could access the deep shafts. Later it was used to feed copper-rich waters into precipitation pools where the copper could be recovered.

On the mountain's southern slope can still be found the precipitation pound, sluice gates and water channels filled with the red water rich in copper. The copper was extracted from the pounds by placing iron objects which caused the copper to precipitate. The mixture of rust and copper precipitated in the pounds could also be used to make a paint known as yellow ochre.

The lunar landscape of the mountain is attractive to visitors because of its rainbow colours, but care must be taken as many shafts are unmarked. Exploring the mountain is best conducted by sticking to the paths. Interest in exploiting the mountain's mineral wealth has been awakened by an increase in the price of metals.

THE GROWTH OF AMLWCH

Before the discovery of copper on Parys Mountain Amlwch was merely a fishing hamlet, but a description in an anonymously published book "A History of Anglesey" in 1775, shows that by then the harbour was much frequented by small sloops, and that the village of Amlwch, half a mile from the shore, had a considerable market on Fridays and a cattle fair on November 12.

Before copper mining on Parys Mountain had transformed Amlwch into a flourishing town, the only shop recorded is the general store belonging to Ann Williams, but as Amlwch was then only a hamlet, the one shop was probably sufficient for the needs of the district.

This small fishing village grew very quickly into an industrial town, which in 1801 was the largest town in North Wales, with a population of nearly 5,000, and the third largest in Wales, housing a wild, heavy drinking mining community, although in fairness it must be said that Arthur Aikin, a traveller who visited Amlwch on a summer Sunday evening described the peaceful scene of groups of men, women and children in their Sunday best enjoying the warmth of a summer evening, with the men reading newspapers and discussing their content, without any of the gross and riotous delight of holiday evenings near the capital. He was at Amlwch on two busy market days and witnessed no drunkeness or quarrelling. He attributed this peaceful scene to the fact that most of the population were Methodists.

Most descriptions of Amlwch at this time were not as idyllic, but Aikin was comparing Amlwch with the industrial towns of England, and the influence of Methodism did create a sense of morality and society that might otherwise have been lacking.

By 1831 the population rose to a high point of 6,285, a fraction more than Cardiff at the time.

This sudden growth resulted in numerous social problems. The small, unhealthy dwellings became overcrowded, and the dirty narrow streets were conducive to the spread of illnesses such as smallpox and typhus, and increased mortality, especially among infants. Although the mines created employment, the influx of people created problems, and at times when the mines were not flourishing unemployment and its attendant problems would rise. A particularly bad time was after the end of the Napoleonic Wars, when former Amlwch men returned after being discharged from employment in Liverpool, and demobilised ex-Amlwch miners also returned to the area. The marquess of Anglesey did try to relieve this by ordering that jobs should be found for the local unemployed, much to the indignation of the stewards.

In addition the herring fishing that year had also been unsuccessful, so that the result of all this unemployment was that the poor rate, whichone in six were already unable to pay was raised further.

The problems caused by unemployment due to returning soldiers and the slump in the mining industry were further exacerbated by the fact that the wet summer of 1816 which resulted in a late harvest with a yield of oats well below the average. The price of bread rose and in 1817 starvation was widespread among the poorer classes across in other parts of Wales.

Sometime in early January 1817 a Vestry meeting was held in Amlwch to consider buying a quantity of corn which would be sold to the poor at cost price when it was scarce. According to William Hughes of Madyn Dusw, it was decided at this meeting to provide £300 for this purpose, and to seek loans of £1,000 from each of the proprietors of the copper mines, but unfortunately the proposals were not carried out vigorously. The lower classes now began to suspect that only a small quantity of inferior corn would be bought for them while the best corn would be exported. This suspicion turned into a fear of an approaching famine, which may have been exaggerated, as one magistrate had told the Plas Newydd Estate controlling agent that there was not the least cause to anticipate a scarcity on the island, although another magistrate, namely the Rev H Wynne Jones, of Trefiorwerth, Bodedern, strongly disagreed.

Matters came to a head on Tuesday, January 28, 1817. The townspeople had warned corn factors about exporting to Liverpool, and converged on the flat Wellington, which was loaded with oats and oatmeal. They removed the ship's rudder and buried it in the churchyard.

In order to allay this discontent, the most respectable of the parish met in the evening at Tymawr. They agreed to raise £300 for purchasing corn and potatoes, and also sent for James Treweek, chief manager of the Mona Mine, and Stephen Roose. The two mining officials were attacked for not helping earlier, and it was widely felt that the £300 which they now offered was very inadequate. The sum considered necessary was £2,000 but despite the prospect of earning interest on this loan, the mine proprietors could not be persuaded to advance more. This hostility between the parish and the mines, which was one of the features of the Amlwch riots, was already being formed.

The employers were unaware of the extreme urgency of the problem. For a number of days after the first outbreak of violence, a mob paraded the town's streets. On February 3, two magistrates, the Rev H Wynne Jones, and Mr Jones of Tyn-y-Coed, Holyhead, arrived at Amlwch, and quickly swore in about 30 special constables.

The magistrates proceeded to take the rudder back to the vessel, but the intimidation offered to the special constables, hindered them from being able to procure any aid in retrieving the rudder, even though no acts of violence were committed, and the unruly, abusive mobs were a few scores of women and children. They were however not abusive to the magistrates.

The special constables sworn in soon disappeared except for five or six, of whom all but one were totally inactive. In such circumstances the magistrates were only able to arrest the ringleader and two others who were particularly active in taking the rudder away. These men offered no resistance, but because of the lack of cooperation from the special constables sworn in, nobody could be obtained to help the constable, so two of the men had to be released on bail.

The ringleader would also have escaped as easily had not William Jones of Amlwch, surgeon volunteered his assistance to the constable, and also prevailed on Henry Hughes, son of the late William Hughes, Parys Lodge to accompany him. By then it was getting dark, and the mob around the inn door had increased considerably and was getting turbulent. The magistrates had to employ a stratagem to take the prisoner away

The following day the rabble tried to rescue the prisoner as he was being marched through Llannerchymedd , on the way to be tried at Beaumaris, but thanks to the help of local special constables, the escort was able to hold back the mob as the prisoner was put on a chaise bound for Beaumaris.

Later the same day an attempt was made to move the ship, but the people who moved the rudder from the churchyard were pelted with stones and pieces of slag.

On hearing the news of this second debacle, the Rev Wynne Jones, who had by then returned to

Treiorwerth, felt obliged to ask the Marquess of Anglesey for military assistance.

It was two weeks before soldiers arrived. During this time the mobs held nightly demonstrations and intimidated several residents, and also laid down conditions for the return of the rudder, but the Rev Wynne Jones was in no mood for compromise.

The Marquess of Anglesey warned the magistrates of the expense of calling out the local militia, and expressed the hope that it was still possible to avoid the disgrace of having regular soldiers at Amlwch.

Meanwhile James Treweek and others who were anxious to avoid the unpleasant necessity of soldiers, had called a meeting for February 18 to consider the case of the unemployed. On that day it was decided to raise a subscription-loan of about £300 for the purpose of putting men to work on harbour improvements. Another £80 or £100 was also felt to be necessary for the upkeep of the public roads, but it was agreed that only a Vestry meeting could sanction this method of helping the poor.

While these matters were being discussed, Lord Whitfield in Dublin Castle had received notice from the deputy lieutenant of Anglesey of further trouble at Amlwch, and on the evening of February 18, 164 men of the 45th Regiment, under Major Alexander Martin, were dispatched for Holyhead. They arrived at Holyhead the following day to the surprise of the Marquess of Anglesey . After a day's rest the soldiers completed their march to Amlwch in less than eight hours, and within two hours of their arrival the captain of the Wellington was able to fix the rudder to the ship.

Although the town remained peaceful during the night, the disposition of the people was such that the three magistrates, Wynne Jones, Hampton and Jones, considered it necessary to keep the soldiers in the town for a week to 10 days. Suitable accommodation was hard to find for the men of the 45th Regiment, so they were quartered at a number of centres. Nevertheless their presence in the town on February 21 enabled the magistrates to take depositions of witnesses, and the captain to load his ship.

The mob could do nothing more than to threaten revenge on the magistrates and corn factors once the troops had departed.

The ship sailed on February 23, and the magistrates turned to the task of securing the peace of the town. Within a few days the Rev H Wynne Jones had helped to seize four rioters, and on March 1 set about strengthening the civil power by directing that respectable residents of the town and nearby areas should serve as special constables to patrol the area. By the end of March a large number of people had been enrolled for this work but the magistrates considered that it would be wise to establish a loyal association at Amlwch.

Once the need for troops had diminished the publicans began to complain about overcrowding. For this reason the Rev H Wynn Jones directed on March 1 that about 40 soldiers should march to Llannerchymedd. On March 7 the main part of the regiment departed for Holyhead, leaving nine officers and 30 privates. Despite pressure from the Marquess of Anglesey, this detachment did not finally leave the area until March 29.

The prospect of the troops' withdrawal led to people looking again at the character of the island's military forces. The Anglesey Regiment of Light Infantry then numbered 102 men while the local militia numbered 29 officers and 70 privates. The militia's commander complained that he had been deprived for months of materials for the militia, and resented the insinuation that the militia would have been ineffective in suppressing disturbances amongst its own people.

The Rev Wynne Jones argued that no dependence could be placed on the militia when the men would be expected to fight their own neighbours and possibly kinsfolk, very likely on such a small island.

The Marquess disagreed, and contrary to his earlier declaration, he now wanted to strengthen the local forces, and was prepared to support the formation of a local volunteer cavalry, so as to avoid the disgrace of another invasion. Ironically the government had already decided to allow militia forces throughout Britain to run down.

Effort to bolster the civil power were accompanied by a greater concern for the welfare of the poorer classes. The Bishop of Bangor offered £20 towards the relief of the poor and also promised to contribute to the improvements in the port which began on March 5.

Another subscription started for clothing the poor, and a rate was levied for the repair of parish roads. Loads of corn which had been bought by the wealthier people, arrived in Amlwch in March and April. Meanwhile several more ringleaders had been apprehended by the local constables, and these appeared at the spring assizes on April 15 and 16. Three of them were convicted and two acquitted, while the rest escaped trial because the prosecutors felt that the legal costs involved were too high. Since the "outrage" of January 28 occurred before the magistrates arrived to read the Riot Act, these costs fell entirely on the people injured by the detention of the vessel, and they would have reason to fear that an Anglesey jury might find the rioters not guilty.

A year later the Rev Wynne Jones unsuccessfully tried to persuade the government to defray the sum of £76 11/8 which had been expended.

Although the Amlwch riots were by far the greatest disturbances in Anglesey in the early 19th century and the first time in 22 years that the magistrates had to call on military assistance, the violence bore all the hallmarks of a typical corn riot. The loeer orders were motivated by a fear of scarcity rather than actual starvation. The price of corn peaked in the summer, not in the early spring. The actions of the rioters showed a concern with maintaining their accustomed diet, and showed a lack of interest in political and industrial matters, but simply in obtaining justice .Their real enemies were not the employers and magistrates, but the farmers who withheld the corn, and the factors who attemted to export it at a profit. The rioters included a wide cross section of the people and enjoyed widespread support, though it must be said that the miners generally played the part of sympathetic onlookers.

The economic grievances which had led to the food riots eased later the same year as the value of copper recovered.

It was only a few people who really prospered, as the majority lived and worked in squalid conditions. Drunkenness, gambling and violence all flourished, as ironic consequences of poor working conditions, long hours, and low wages. In the light of such poverty parents could ill-afford not to send their children to work so very few of the really poor attended school before the mid 19th century. The 1847 survey of education in Wales paints a vivid picture of this poverty, with the streets of Amlwch consisting of rows of cottages or hovels of the lowest description, destitute of proper light or ventilation . Parents who were unable to clothe their children properly were content for them to beg for whatever extra money they could muster.

These conditions presented a direct challenge to religious leaders and educationalists alike. According to the Rev William Roberts, a much respected Methodist minister in the locality, there was "not a place in the country where there are so many children uneducated".

Bingley, who was travelling through Wales, commented that Amlwch was "entirely dependent for its prosperity on the copper mines, for most of its inhabitants have some concern in them, either as miners or agents." Suddenly it became a prosperous market town with shops and its own brewery and some small industries.

Aikin, writing in 1797, said "The town of Amlwch which about 30 years ago had no more than half a dozen houses in the whole parish now supports a population of four or five thousand".

This rapid growth brought its problems. James Treweek, the Cornish mine agent whose family was to play a large part in the industrial history of the town, stated "Amlwch is one of the worst places I ever knew for young men to be brought up in ... because of the many pot houses in the town and the company who attend them regularly".

The state of the medical services available in the town at the time was also a cause for worry. The Mona Mines MSS has a comment on the town's medical profession: "There are three doctors at Amlwch. One is a drunkard, the second lacks experience and surgical skill and the third is habitually in the same condition as the first".

These comments can be understood when one remembers that at the time of writing this comment there were no fewer than 60 public houses in Amlwch.

AMLWCH PORT

The existence of a natural harbour in the location of today's Amlwch Port helped the development of commercial mining operations.

The commercial exploitation of the copper on Parys Mountain started in1768, and by 1770 over 20 vessels, including some form as far as Aberystwyth, Aberdyfi and Liverpool were engaged in the transport of copper, and between March 1771 and March 1772, 2,475 tons of ore were taken from Amlwch to the Warrington Copper and Brass company.

The development kept pace with the increase in mining operations, but no real effort was made to improve and enlarge the natural harbour until the end of the 18th century . In 1783 an Act of Parliament was passed for this purpose. In 1782 the Paeys Mining Company built a small pier when it realised that better facilities would be realised to handle cargoes, and in 1793 an Act was passed to enlarge, deepen, cleanse and improve the harbour which allowed shelter for 30 sloops from 60 to 100 tons.

Illustration 4: An old print of the entrance to Amlwch harbour (Public domain)
The growth of the port also led to a growth of a shipbuilding industry at Amlwch Port, and also in nearby Cemaes Bay.

In 1817 a small lighthouse was built 28 feet above half-tide level on a stone pier.

Illustration 5: This lighthouse guided ships into the safety of the small creek

In 1827 storm force winds drove the sea up to the neck of the harbour, and the same year, in order to lessen the damage to ships within the harbour during northerly gales, great beams of timber, some 13 in number, were let down into grooves cut in the harbour walls. The grooves and the inner sea gate may still be seen and with a little imagination one can visualise the hustle and bustle of the days when up to 30 ships would be laid up to the harbour walls, awaiting the arrival of red copper ore.

At the same time regulations were strictly enforced regarding entering and leaving the port, which involved the crews of visiting vessels manhandling the baulks, a practice unpopular from its inception.

With the decline of the copper industry from the middle of the 19th century the fortunes of the port also declined, as did the population of the town. The coming of the railways with cheaper freight charges than those by sea also hastened the decline of the port. During this decline Amlwch became a small but popular yachting harbour and tourist destination.

The decline led to unemployment, and to the deterioration of the disused harbour building, and it was only in recent years that an interest in the past has led to regeneration and conservation of the port area.

Today the port area is somewhat of an open air museum with many buildings, such as dry docks, copper ore bins and a windmill, dating from the port's copper exporting day, and the Copper Kingdom museum housed in the Sail Loft brings to life the days when this was a hive of industry. The three-storey watch tower on the end of the intermediate pier bears an 1853 date stone, and in the past alerted the harbour crews of approaching vessels, and served as a kind of lighthouse.

Illustration 6: Present day view of the port area with a museum housed in one of the old warehouses
The harbour is still in use, but now berthing the tugs that service the oil tankers that now moor near the coast.

In 1872 an Anglican church was built in Amlwch Port.

SHIPBUILDING

A growing port meant a demand for ships, and a shipbuilding industry in Amlwch and nearby Cemaes Bay, and in the case of Amlwch the copper stained water, a by-product of th copper industry, was good for treating ship timbers.

In the 1820s James Treweek's sons formed the Anglesey Shipbuilding Company, which built small cutters and larger vessels of up to 200 tons, and repair work was also carried out. During the early 19th century shipbuilding was largely a monopoly of the Treweek family, who were still regarded as foreigners despite having been in Amlwch for some time.

In 1860 Captain William Thomas of Bryn Eilian acquired the Treweeks' shipyards, and as this coincided with a number of favourable events, his business was successful. During 1858-70 the Parys Mountain Copper mines enjoyed a revival, Hill's Chemical plant was established in Amlwch, and ships were needed for the expanding North Wales resorts and Liverpool.

Amlwch's craftsmen, especially joiners and craftsmen, were renowned, and their work was in great demand with Liverpool firms, and many of the builders in Liverpool were from Anglesey and had come on Amlwch ships.

In 1867 the Anglesey Central railway reached Amlwch, and offered an alternative means of transport, and the decline of the copper industry also meant the decline of the port, but the shipbuilding industry of William Thomas and Son continued to flourish during the 1880s. The last ship built my William Thomas and Son was the motor schooner Eilian, built in 1908 was the first of her size to be designed with an internal combustion engine. William Thomas and son finally closed in 1951.

Some of the three masted schooners traded between South America and the Gulf of Finland, and some had remarkable careers as Q ships in the First World Wars.

OTHER INDUSTRIES

The growth of the copper and shipping industries led to the growth of other trades which serviced these industries and their workers. These included smiths, leather workers, carpenters and sailmakers. General stores and public houses doubling as inns also flourished.

The byproducts created by the copper industry meant that chemical industries could flourish. These included ochre pigments, sulphur, vitriol and alum.

Perhaps it should not come as too much of a surprise in an industrial community, with a hard-drinking population that there was a brewery at Amlwch port, and that clog-making and tobacco processing were other notable industries at Amlwch.

The Amlwch Brewery is shown on a map of Amlwch Port as early as 1780, in the square just above the port. In 1828 the Francis map still showed the presence of the larger brewery on the square, but also that the Marquess of Anglesey had a smaller brewery on Lower Quay Street. There was also a brewery associated with the Dinorben Arms, and in 1890 the OS map showed the Parys Brewery.

The tobacco industry was already in existence in Amlwch as early as 1844, when Morgan and Jones, tobacco manufacturer is listed in the Slaters Directory. The company continued to produce its own tobacco brands until the late 1940s, and remained in business until 1985.

Other tobacco companies in Amlwch were Edward Morgan Hughes in Methusalem Street, and William Mostyn (which changed its name to Hugh Owen and Son by 1910). The types of tobacco produced were snuff, twist and shag.

Other industries, much more common throughout Anglesey include fulling mills and windmills, and Amlwch is typical of Anglesey in this respect.

A fulling mill called Pandy was known to be in operation in 1776. And the existence of Cae'r Pandy suggests that there was a fulling mill there.

Amlwch Port windmill was built in 1816 and was still standing in 1929. There was also a windmill on Parys Mountain, which was built in 1878, and still standing in 1929. The Parys Mountain windmill was unusual in that it was the only one in Anglesey with five sails, and was used for pumping water from the mine shafts rather than the more usual purpose of grinding corn.

In the light of the prominence of the chemical industry in Amlwch during the heyday of the Parys mines, it should be no surprise that chemical industries should play a prominent part in more recent times as well.

In the early days of motoring poor quality fuels were a problem, and in 1920 it was found that a chemical called Tetraethyl Lead was good at preventing the problem of engines "knocking", but this had the side-effect of creating a build-up of lead in the engine. Another chemical, called Dibromoethane, was effective at preventing this build-up.

In 1953 a bromine and Dibromoethane plant, run by the Associated Ethyl Company Limitedwas sited at Amlwch. Bromine is extracted from the sea, and the seawater needs to be as clean as possible, replenished with fresh seawater, and warmed by the Gulf Stream. All these factors favoured Amlwch for the plant's location. In 1961 the company changed its name to Associated Octel Company Limited.

This company was based for many years almost solely on the production of anti-knock chemicals, but the introduction of unleaded petrol in the 1980s reduced the demand for these.

In the late 1990s the Amlwch site was taken over by Great Lakes Chemicals Limited, and switched to producing bromine for a wide range of other products, but the cost of raw materials and of transport meant that the plant closed in 2005.

In 2008 another company, Canatxx, expressed an interest in the old Octel plant, for Liquid Natural Gas gasification plant, but the plan has not yet come into fruition.

Other industries include Budenberg Gauges which was at Amlwch from 1962-1990, and Rehau, a German plastic parts company which set up in Amlwch in 1974.

OIL

During the 1960s the Stanlow Oil Refinery in Cheshire was finding difficulties with crude oil supplies, as the new supertankers had difficulties with restrictions placed due to the busy nature of the Mersey, and in trying to moor off Stanlow.

A solution to this was to have a floating oil receiving station built off Amlwch, where ships could moor in deep waters, and the oil could then be pumped to a terminal at Rhosgoch,and then to the Stanlow refinery, through miles of underground pipelines, well concealed, so as not to spoil the landscape.

From 1974 when the first tanker was unloaded at Amlwch, the plant received oil tankers from various parts of the world, and in 1981 the two largest tankers in the world, both of 550 , 0000 tons, berthed there. From Amlwch the crude oil was pumped to the oil terminal at Rhosgoch, and then to the Stanlow refinery in Cheshire, through miles of underground pipelines which which are well concealed so as not to spoil the landscape.

By the mid 1980s the use of large crude oil tankers was diminishing, and the plant closed in 1990.

Although this work was relatively short-lived, many communities still benefit from the Isle of Anglesey Charitable Trust, which was founded through negotiation with Shell.

POSTAL SERVICES

In 1822 Thomas Telford's new main road across Anglesey was completed, so the Gwyndu inn, in Llandrygarn was no longer on the main postal route. The Marquess of Anglesey and several Amlwch residents had requested the establishment of a private coach service from Amlwch to connect with the Holyhead to London mailcoach at Mona Inn, on Thomas Telford's new road, near Llangefni. John Hughes, the enterprising landlord of the Glazier's Arms, Amlwch, agreed to run a light coach with two good horses along this route daily, provided that the allowances on the Mona Mine bags and the pence on the other letters be transferred to him from the postmistress of Gwyndy. The Post Office authorities, however, rejected the scheme because of the state of the road from Llangefni through Llannerchymedd. Undeterred, John Hughes put forward another proposal, to run his coach from Amlwch along the old line of road to Bangor Ferry to meet the Liverpool packet boats. But this, like his first proposal, met little encouragement, as it was contrary to the strict regulations of the Post Office to furnish bags or letters to be delivered to stagecoaches

In October 1826 it was announced that the Bangor penny post area was to be expanded so that it would include a large area of Anglesey including Amlwch. The first appointed Penny Post receiver at Amlwch was Thomas Jones, landlord of the King's Head, and the office was located in his tavern in King Street. In 1838 he was succeeded by Samuel Judd, a builder, who held the post for over 30 years, first at Methusalem Street, and later at Petters Street.

EDUCATION

AMLWCH FREE SCHOOL

During the 1650s a school was set up in Amlwch (one of 60 established in Wales between 1650 and 1653 under an Act of Parliament which was designed to advance education and piety). Little is known for certain about the school, and there is much uncertainty about the date of its founding with one author being of the opinion that there was a school in Amlwch before 1646.

One proof that there was a school there before 1650 occurs in a dictionary of biography of clergy of Bangor Diocese, where it is said that "Lewis John, son of Howel Lewis of Anglesey. Educated at Amlwch School, and St John's Cantab: BA 1650, MA 1654, 1655 R (ector) Llanfaethlu.

The school had one schoolmaster who earned £20 per annum, and although there is no specific evidence relating to Amlwch Free School, itis interesting that girls as well as boys were educated in similar schools.

It is likely that Greek and Latin, corresponding to the curriculum in English schools, were the subjects taught in the Free School. The school was free to children of all classes, and the Puritan influence was heavy with the great emphasis placed on the Bible and the preacher-like attitude of the schoolmasters. This may explain the short existence of these schools.

It was expected that the schoolmasters should obtain a licence from the bishop, a practice that went back as far as the Middle Ages. It is unknown how long the Amlwch Free School lasted, but most of the 60 schools established under the 1650 Act were closed before the Restoration around 1662.

CHARITY SCHOOL

After the free school's short existence in the 17th century we don't hear of another school in the parish until the end of the century.

The only hope the poor had of having an education at that time an up to as late as the mid 19th century was the charity schools.

Many of these charity schools were endowed by wealthy people. In the case of Amlwch it was a widow from London who provided the means for education. On September 24, 1689 Eleanor Kynnier made a will endowing £311 in a trust intended for providing a school for the poor children of the parish to teach them to read and write.

An agreement was signed appointing Richard Bulkeley, Glan y Gors, and Robert Bulkeley, London, Gent, to be responsible for investing the money by buying lands and properties in Anglesey, and using the rents and profits from these – two thirds to maintain a school for boys and the rest for a school for girls.

In 1704, John Owen, the schoolmaster, received a salary of £7 12/6 (£7.62) per annum, while the schoolmistress Gloria Hughes received £3 12/6.

Because of a lack of cooperation among the trustees, no school at all was kept in the period 1706 to 1723. At that time a young man, aged 21 years called Owen Bulkeley received a licence to keep a school in the town. Keeping a school without a licence from the bishop was then a punishable offence.

It is not known how effective Owen was as a schoolmaster, but the remarks by William Morris of the Morris brothers regarding some of the clerics of his time, certainly do not reflect at all well on his quality as a priest.

"They are no better than Owain Bulkeley Glan y traeth, the biggest idiot that ever wore a surplice, who drinks the health of the devil, because if there were no devil there would be no need for priests."

Owen was from Gronant, Llanfachraeth, and his brother John kept a school in Llanfechell.

During the period 1699-1740 the Society for the Propagation of Christian Knowledge was active in publishing books, mostly Bibles and The Book of Common Prayer, in Welsh, and distributing them freely across Wales, and establishing schools to teach the princples of Christianity according to the Church of England. A prominent member of the society in Anglesey was Dr John Jones, Dean of Bangor, who sponsored schools in Llangeinwen, Beaumaris, Llanfihangel Ysgeifiog, Pentraeth and Rhoscolyn.

The Amlwch Charity School did not belong to the SPCK, the schoolmaster received twice the salary received by schoolmasters employed by the SPCK. In the light of this it is difficult to understand why the school was not run at Amlwch between 1689 and 1727.

Owen Bulkeley moved from Amlwch where he received a salary of £8 per annum as a schoolmaster to become a curate in Llanddeusant receiving £16.

There were some difficulties regarding the school's money in 1769. The church wardens went to

Llanidan at a cost of 2/6 (12.5 pence) to claim the money, and then to Caernarfon and to the court (brawdlys) in Beaumaris. In 1770 the legal services of Thomas Williams of Llanidan (known as the copper king and Twm Chwarae Teg) to claim successfully thedue money,which amounted to £8 14/6 (£8.72).

In 1786 £300 from the charity was invested on tolls on some of the tollbooths between Porthaethwy and Holyhead.

The parish of Amlwch could boast of having had a school which provided some kind of education for over a century, but with periods when no school was held at all, and some periods when the charity funding was misused.

In 1801 no master was appointed at Amlwch because the majority of the trustees were deceased, and although the school appeared to thrive a decade later, in 1814 the return stated that the school had not been kept for some time. It has to be said that although in theory this charity was intended to provide an educaation for the children of the poor, in practice the truly poor were more concerned with getting their children to earn their keep, than with providing an education to ensure a more prosperous future.

The endowment of this dormant educational charity was transferred in 1823 to the National School which was struggling with financial difficulties.

CIRCULATING SCHOOLS

The circulating schools, as the name suggests were set up as temporary schools by Griffth Jones, during the second half of the 18th century, with the aim of teaching reading and writing so that the pupils would be able to read theBible for themselves. In the parish of Amlwch these schools were held at Pilwrn, Trogog Uchaf and Bodhunod, during the 1770s and also at Llaneilian parish church.

NATIONAL SCHOOL

The growth of the industrial proletariat in the area, coupled with the dormant nature of the educational endowment which had been established by Eleanor Kynnier, led to the need for a public charity school for Amlwch to be considered a matter of urgency.

At a Vestry meeting in October 1816 it was resolved that the churchwardens should be called on to revive the school established by Eleanor Kynnier. However, as nothing was being done, several inhabitants called a meeting on April 6, 1818 to consider establishing a National School.

With almost £200 in accumulated interest to hand, the erection of a capacious school for 200 children, at a cost not exceeding £250 seemed feasible.

However, months passed without any further progress until a meeting was summoned at Beaumaris on September 29, 1819. This time it was decided to invest the endowment in Government securities, apply to the Marquess of Anglesey for land on which to build the school, and to invite financial support from the proprietors of the Mona and Parys Mines.

During the next few month the Bishop of Bangor made representations to the Marquess of Anglesey and the two companies, which resulted in the acquisition of a site, a liberal donation of £100 from each company, and the promise of an annual subscription of £25 towards the maintenance of the school.

The Bishop had made it plain from the start that he did not approve of the plan for the proposed school, as he considered it an "unsightly scheme" and potentially expensive.

It was not long before his fears were realised, as the expense of the building far outstripped the estimate.

The school cost £1,015 to build, and received a National Society grant of £200.

Despite these financial difficulties the National School opened on December 19, 1821, with Thomas Jones as the schoolmaster. Within a few months he had good reason to regret his appointment, as he wrote a letter to the Marquess of Anglesey's steward, complaining that his salary had not been paid because the school funds were entirely exhausted and the institution several hundreds of pounds in debt, and even the buildings were in a very incomplete state.

As there was not much chance of the financial situation being remedied, he sought permission to levy a penny per week from each of the pupils in lieu of a salary. There were almost 180 pupils at the school, all in a "fine state of submission and making very rapid progress in learning". In addition another 20 were about to start attending the school, and there were 130 in the girls' school.

Forced by necessity, the managers appealed to the National Society for more aid for the school in

June 1822. Their request was based on the fact that most of the parents were miners employed at the Parys Copper Mines, who were unable to pay for the education of their children.

Although a grant of £100 was obtained, a deficiency of £365 still remained. The managers decided in August to approach the trustees of Eleanor Kynnier's charity, so that they might use the accumulated interest of the fund towards liquidating the debt. This endowment was transferred to the National School in 1823.

However, this was not sufficient, so the managers directed appeals to various entrepreneurs with business connections to Amlwch. This proved successful, with donations and subscriptions being received from companies such as the coal suppliers Gaunt & Co of Llanelli, and the great copper middlemen Newton, Lyon & Co, of Liverpool.

Even so, the school building remained unfinished as late as January 1824, and the shortage of funds meant that the pupils were always ill-provided for books and pencils.

The National School in Amlwch, like almost all schools in Anglesey, was condemned in the report published in 1847, and had been under a cloud since then, but nothing was done to remedy the situation until 1853. The report complained that not only the floors, walls and windows were dirty, vut that neither the furniture or the rooms were even washed or swept.

The Diocesan Inspector, roused by the prospect of a rival British School, removed the existing untrained master, and also tried to balk the establishment of the rival school by enlisting the support of C H Evans, the Plas Newydd agent.

Declaring himself to be no "bigoted churchman", but a practical educationalist, he warned that competition in Amlwch would only degenerate into unhealthy opposition. Each school would strive to give education at the cheapest rate and least amount of discipline, whilst the children would be brought up in hatred of each other.

Amlwch National School remained a voluntary (non-provided) school on June 1, 1904.

BRITISH SCHOOL

Plans were proposed for a British School in 1853, and as we have seen in the last chapter, the Diocesan Inspector had tried to stop these plans being realised.

Despite these machinations, a site was eventually secured for the British School in the centre of the town. To all appearances, the movement had only been kept alive by the vision and zeal of a single Methodist minister, the Rev William Roberts, then aged 72. Having received only three months of formal education he was personally fitted to appreciate the value of education.

Moreover, as a Dissenter, he was determined to see the establishment of an unsectarian school in the community, where children need not fear the rod each Monday for neglecting the church. In October 1858, as an acknowledgement of his leadership, William Roberts was given the honour of laying the foundation stone of the new school.

This school was established in 1860 and opened on March 26, 1860, and cost £2,500. It had received a Treasury grant of £1,146.

Few British Schools had an annual income equal to that of a National School, and in October 1860 the Rev William Roberts complained that the road to solvency remained as dark as ever. Racked by recurrent financial troubles, the committee decided in 1863, not only to raise the school fees, but also to seek patronage from Plas Newydd.

Although this appeal was sternly opposed by T Fanning Evans, the Plas Newydd agent, who claimed that the school had been built for "no other purpose than to gratify the party spirit of a certain clique", an annual subscription of £10 was authorised.

By the 1870s the British School had been in financial difficulties for a number of years. Attempts were made to impose a cheaper voluntary rate in 1876 and 1879. But in spite of the most strenuous efforts, too many people had defaulted, and in 1882, when the deficiency stood at £96, the managers were obliged to call for the formation of a school board, which was formed on February 27 1883, and comprised buth Amlwch and Rhosybol British Schools. Both Amlwch and Rhosybol British Schools remained under the board until 1895, when Rhosybol became a separate board district.

PRIVATE SCHOOLS

Amlwch, like many other places, had several private schools over the years.

The first listed in David Pretty's book Two Centuries of Anglesey Schools, was that run by Robert Hughes (Robin Ddu o Fon) before 1763, and in around 1802 Mrs Martin held a Dame School.

During the early 19th century many Dissenting ministers ran schools as a sideline, one of which was run by Independent minister Rev John Evans between 1795-1807, and another Independent Minister, William Jones in 1826. Another of these "preacher-teachers" was Thomas Jones, Amlwch, who was the author of many Welsh books on religion, geography and arithmetic. In addition to preaching with the Methodists, he had contacted schools at Bodedern and Amlwch.

In 1811 the populous town of Amlwch had two or three little schools, supported by anything teachers can procure for their pains. One such school was kept in 1817 by a certain John Thomas. Owing to a defect in his left arm he was unable to do any physical work; consequently he had opened a small school in the town which was attended by 10 scholars who paid him 3 shillings a quarter. Cornelius Pritchard, another schoolmaster at Amlwch in 1820, conducted a school because he had not been brought up to any other employment than that of using the pen.

To meet the needs of the "better class" children in Amlwch, a private school had been set up by 1814, which offered instruction in spelling, writing and reading at seven shillings and sixpence a quarter, and more advanced subjects at correspondingly higher fees.

William Francis ran a well respected school at Amlwch for over 40 years, and in the 1851 census he was enumerated as "Teacher of Navigation". He seems a very interesting character. He was pressed by his wife to forsake a perilous naval career in 1813, during the Napoleonic War, as he was about to sail to Gibraltar. He opted for the sedentary (but less profitable) life of a school teacher, opening his academy in January 1814. As might be expected, his curriculum was heavily slanted towards mathematics, geography, navigation and nautical studies. In 1821 he applied unsuccessfully to the local Plas Newydd agent for permission to convert the old Assay Office into a schoolroom. With the fine view of the horizon he would have been in a better position to explain Hadley's Quadrant and other nautical and astronomical instruments to his pupils.

Through the patronage of Col Hughes MP, he was able to secure a large house called Mount Pleasant in 1824, and here, punctuated by moments when he considered abandoning his school altogether, he remained until his death in 1853. According to his obituary, he was unrivalled as a teacher of mathematics and navigation.

Some of the episodes when he was considering giving up were in July 1828 and March 1829. In July 1828 he wrote a letter to Sanderson seeking employment in one of the Mine offices. He complained that one of the reasons for his diminished earnings was the seminaries run by the preachers of the various denominations, who through the influence they had on their congregations, were able to attract of most parents who were above sending their children to the National School. The fact that these teachers received annual stipends from their respective congregations meant that they were able to fix lower fees than was possible for him, and the love of novelty drew pupils into their schools.

Although John Sellers commenced his Academy for Young Gentlemen a few years before Francis's death, he is generally regarded as the old schoolmaster's successor. At both establishments the respective wives conducted a separate department for young ladies; Sellers took particular care to point out that in his school the two rooms were "quite distinct". Like his predecessor, he too dedicated 40 years to his profession. This school for young ladies and gentlemen was held at Glanyrafon Academy, Queen Street and Salem Street from May 1849 until 1889.

The quality of the schools were quite varied. Many were the so-called Dame Schools, which were private elementary schools at the lower end of the spectrum, usually taught by women at their own homes, while other schools had much higher aspirations. Although there were seven private schools in Amlwch, many of these were little better than the National Schools which were making headway in the county.

The schools listed in David Pretty's book Two Centuries of Anglesey Schools, include the following: the school run by Cornelius Pritchard in around 1820; Carmel School, a Dame School in existence during 1827-46; the Glanrafon Academy run by W Gregson during 1831-35, which offered board and education at £20 per year; a school at Rhosybol run by the Rev Robert Williams (Calvinistic Methodist) in around 1833; a Dame School run by a Miss Jones from 1836-46; a school run by a Miss Anwyl in 1840; one in Queen Street, run by a Miss Clarke in 1844; a dame school run by a Miss Griffiths in 1846-7; a day school run by Edward and Martin Kennedy of King Street in 1850; a school run by Mary Francis during 1856-1880 at King Street and Salem Street; a school kept at King Street by Phoebe Hughes during 1856-61; a school for young ladies and gentlemen kept by Mr and Mrs W G Treweek of Glanyrafon during 1866-68; a school at Tredath, kept by Miss Charlotte Andrew at Tredath, during 1866-83 teaching English and music; a day school for young ladies kept by Mrs W H Larkin at Shopgron House in 1874; Mona House School in Petter's Street, kept by Mr and Mrs Hobday during 1877-86, which was described as a first class Private School teaching English and accomplishments; a school at Peniel Chapel kept by a Mrs Jones in 1881; the "University School" kept by Mr Noall during 1881-1890, teaching mercantile, classical, mathematical and scientific subjects; boys' private school at Western Terrace, Tredath run by Mr J Owen during 1881-86; a boarding and day school run by James Skelton during 1890, which provided a commercial education.

In 1877 Mr and Mrs Hobday from Birmingham opened a school at Amlwch at the request of the leading families, who were anxious that their daughters should receive an English education.

Mrs Hobday seems to have discontinued her school in 1884, as in September 1886 she put an announcement in the North Wales Chronicle saying that after two years she now wished, with the assistance of her daughter, to resume the school, offering a thorough English education, and accomplishments including painting, special attention to letter writing and book keeping. In connection with her school, select adult and juvenile dancing classes were offered during the winter months under the tuition of a professional teacher.

Amlwch Port also had private schools during the second half of the 19th century. These included the dame school run by Jane Jones at the Calvinistic Methodist chapel house, during 1850-93; another dame school, which was run by Ann Jones during 1856-59; a school run by Owen Lewis in around 1860; and dame schools run by Mary Rowlands in 1874 and by Miss Leis, Llaneilian Road in 1881-1889.

A Ragged School was established in Amlwch in 1887, and was run by a Mr and Mrs Morgan. It was apparently still in existence in 1901.

RHOSYBOL BRITISH SCHOOL

A British School was in existence at Gorslwyd, Rhosybol as early as 1844. In the Educational Inquiry of 1846-7 it was one of only five British Schools in Anglesey. It seems to have initially been held in a chapel or a cottage. It was certainly mentioned in the 1847 report that it was held in a small cottage, but that a new school building for 200 pupils was nearly ready.

A new British School building was opened in Rhosybol in 1847, at a cost of £191, with a Treasury grant of £200. The report said that newly opened building was in a commendable state.

The schoolmaster at Rhosybol had been to Borough Road College for about four months. His salary of £35 was made up entirely from the children's school pence, which did not make for a secure income in lean years.

As was inevitable in an area described as excessively poor. The committee at Rhosybol found itself in serious financial difficulties within months of the new school opening. Only an earnest appeal for aid from the Marquess of Anglesey saved it from extinction. The position was further improved by an unprecedented agreement with the Rev Morris Williams (Nicander), the High Church curate of Amlwch, whereby for a rent of £20 the committee allowed the school to be used as a place to celebrate divine service on Sundays, the Bishop having licensed the building for the purpose. It seems that a British School committee that lacked the money to pay the master's salary was prepared to consider any means open to them, however bizarre or repugnant it may be.

Rhosybol had a new board school built in June 1901, at a cost of £720. It had been part of the Amlwch School Board along with Amlwch British School, but became separate on May 8, 1896.

COUNTY SCHOOL

Although Amlwch, as one of Anglesey's main towns, had been considered as a possible location for a County School since the 1890s, it was treated as part of the Llangefni catchment area, and only finally opened on April 16, 1940, in temporary premises at the Memorial Institute, a building which incorporated the old British School.

The present school building of Ysgol Syr Thomas Jones (named after Sir Thomas Jones, 1870-1945, a local doctor and champion of the County Council) was opened in1950. The design of the school with wide corridors, and underground tunnels, has been attributed to plans for it to double as a potential wartime hospital.

RELIGION

The religious life of the town dates back to the age of the Saints with an old chapelry called Capel Elaeth, dedicated to Saint Elaeth, which was probably on the site of the present parish church. Unsurprisingly, there was also a well connected to the same saint, Ffynnon Elaeth, which was near the site of the brewery in Amlwch Port in 1920.

Half a mile east of Rhosybol, near Trysglwyn there was another chapelry, called Cappel Tegeryn.

By the end of the 18th century the parish church, St Eleth's, became inadequate for the needs of the parish due to the influx of population resulting from the new copper industry. Church records show that by 1792 a new building was deemed necessary. The mines companies offered a contribution of £600 towards the cost, provided the remainder was met through local rates. But the Bishop of Bangor (who also happened to be rector of Amlwch) disagreed, insisting that the companies should meet the entire cost themselves. It seems that he thought that the companies would be willing to fund a new church at any price.

The death of the Bishop solved this impasse, and the new Bishop consecrated the new edifice in 1800, which although a 19th century building, was in a Neo-Classical style more in keeping with the 18th century. Amlwch was proud of its new church, which had an organ and a choir gallery. The final cost was £2,500 to which the mine owners, the Earl of Uxbridge, the Rev Edward Hughes and Thomas Williams contributed.

The original plan for a church costing £800 was by a Mr Wyatt (presumably the well-known architect James Wyatt). Though Wyatt's original plan was evidently not used, there is some grounds for supposing that the church was built from his design, since its builder, John Dale was for many years employed by Wyatt.

This new parish church clearly had formidable competition for the loyalties of the local population, as the Bishop's Visitation return for Amlwch in 1801 showed that the majority of miners had already turned their backs on the established Church, and the local clergyman confessed that his effort were totally inadequate for checking the growth of Methodism.

From the late 18th century, Nonconformity established itself in Amlwch, with Carmel Independent chapel founded in 1785, Bethel Capel licensed for Protestant Dissenters in 1789, and a thriving Methodist cause.

Methodism came early to Amlwch with preaching at Ty Du, the home of Thomas Phabby. In 1777 he bought a site at Penybontfawr from Herbert Jones of Llynon for £30, which he leased for 999 years at 6d a year to the trustees for the building of Bethesda Calvinistic Methodist chapel.

The general pattern for the growth of Methodism was that "societies" (seiadau) would be formed in the wake of missionary preaching, and these will develop into Sunday schools and then into churches. Such societies were later established at Burwen, and at Amlwch Port.

In 1796 the English scientist Arthur Aikin had visited Amlwch and his favourable description of the behaviour of the inhabitants on a Sunday evening, shows the positive influence Methodism had on the people's conduct.

In 1807 the Calvinistic Methodist chapel was called Capel Mawr, and in 1820 changed its name to

Bethesda. This chapel was rebuilt in 1871. It reverted to Capel Mawr in 1944, and in 1988 changed back to Capel Bethesda. This chapel was rebuilt in 1818, as a large chapel called Capel Mawr.

Illustration 7: Capel Mawr, otherwise known as Bethesda Calvinistic Methodist chapel (Public domain)

This is probably the same chapel as that called Capel Mawr, which was licensed in 1801 as a meeting place for the "Independents" (sometimes, the Calvinistic Methodists were referred to as Independents, a term more usually used for Congregationalists), the same year as another chapel at Rhosybol. We shall discuss the troubled history of the Rhosybol chapel later.

Bethesda's branches included a schoolroom called Llaethdy, which was erected in 1860 and rebuilt in 1905. The schoolroom at Llaethdy Bach was previously held at a place called Carreg Cwrnach. In 1860 a schoolroom or small chapel was built between Llaethdy Bach and Melin Adda, and this schoolroom was called Llaethdy Bach.

During 1813-37 there was another Calvinistic Methodist chapel, called Horeb. This and Salem Chapel had been licensed forMethodists in 1811.

Other chapels licensed during the late 18th and early 19th centuries included: a house called Bethesda licensed in 1794 as a meeting place for Baptists in Amlwch; a house in Bridge Street licensed for Baptists in 1806; a chapel in Burwen licensed for Protestants in 1814; Ty Mawr, licensed for Protestants in 1814.

In 1818 a field known as Parc Bach was licensed as a temporary meeting place for Protestants in Amlwch.

In 1820 the Calvinistic Methodists opened a Sunday school at Amlwch Port, held at the house of David Owen, clogmaker for a year. Within a year it moved to a storehouse near the port, and two years later it moved to a small house near where the later chapel stood. In 1827 a new schoolroom was built. In 1901 a new chapel called Peniel was opened at Amlwch Port.

Burwen Calvinistic Methodist chapel, about a mile and a half from Amlwch on the Cemaes road, started as a Sunday school held at a dwelling called Pig-y-Rhos around 1801.In 1816 the cause moved to a house on the other side of the road, opposite the later chapel. This house was still called Ty'r Ysgol in 1935.

In April 1838 an application for land to establish a Methodist chapel and Sunday school at Burwen was met with approval by the Plas Newydd agent. This approval was quite clearly due to political considerations to secure Methodist votes, as the Plas Newydd Estate appeared more keen to curry favour with the Methodists if an election was looming, but at other times, such as in 1837 when there was an appeal for land for a Methodist chapel in Amlwch , the agent said that he was not bound to assist dissent.

A new chapel was built in 1897, to be replaced by another newer one in 1935.

Peniel, Amlwch Port was established in about 1850. In about 1861 a new chapel was built

According to a Government report in 1833 the Calvinistic Methodists had as many as eight Sunday schools in Amlwch.

A Calvinistic Methodist Chapel was planted at Mynydd Parys in 1884

Amlwch's Roman Catholic church is a pre-war concrete building by the Italian architect Rinvoluccri, in the shape of an upturned boat.

In 1872 an Anglican Church was built in Amlwch Port, and in 1875 at Rhosybol.

RHOSYBOL CALVINISTIC METHODIST CHURCH

The Calvinistic Methodist Church in Rhosybol started after 1791, after two farms were divided into several small holdings for letting out, and one of the new tenants was a John Pritchard, who had come from Llannerchymedd and was a Methodist. His arrival encouraged the two Methodists who already lived in the area, to try to get preaching to take place there, so they acquired a house for this purpose, which was to be later called Capel Bach, but the cause grew so that the Capel Bach was soon too small, and a new chapel was built on another part of the plot.

Through the influence of someone hostile to the Methodists , an order was given for this church to be pulled down. It seems that the parish parson and the estate supervisor were angered at the new chapel. Their opportunity came when John Pritchard was expelled from membership of the Methodist Church for having been drunk at Llannerchymedd fair, and for having neglected Sunday services, and his revenge was to reveal to the supervisor that the chapel was not actually built on his land, but on another site that he later enclosed.

The supervisor took advantage of this information to order the Parys Mountain miners to demolish the chapel and take the seats and pulpit to be auctioned. A godly farmer called Richard William Meredith came forward at the auction and warned everyone not to touch the sacred objects, which disrupted the auction, and nobody bought these fittings.

Richard William Meredith went to Mr Williams, Treban, to get land for a new chapel. After getting land for the new chapel, he had difficulty in obtaining stones, but a Mr Williams , shopkeeper of Llannerchymedd, to Mrs Lloyd of Llwydiarth to get permission to quarry stones on her life.

The cause at Rhosybol was in a low state for some years but in about 1811 or 1812 things started to look up at Gorslwyd as in that year many were added to it. There was a further increase in the wake of a revival in Anglesey, ad the Monthly Meeting brought the revival to Gorslwyd. In 1827 a larger chapel was built.

HEALTH CARE

Anglesey was hit by cholera epidemics durin the 19th century, with outbreaks in 1832, 1849 (with 22 dying at Amlwch in a short period), 1854 and the final one in 1866.

EISTEDDFODAU

The Anglesey county eisteddfod was held in Amlwch in 1865, 1870, 1886, and 1894, and in Amlwch Port in 1887.

AMLWCH AUTHORS

As a town that had grown suddenly in the wake of the copper industry, Amlwch could appear rather devoid of culture, but it would be wrong to yield to the temptation to dismiss it as as a cultural desert, though it does seem that some of the more cultured inhabitants did talk of the town in such terms

The poet Dafydd Ddu Eryri came to Amlwch in 1795 as a coal meter, and stayed there until June 1799. In a letter to Sion Lleyn he longed for the more cultured and literature-loving society in Caernarfonshire, and claimed to have almost lost his poetic gift due to lack of inspiration.

The cleric and poet Rev Morris Williams (who is more generally known by his poetic name Nicander, and is the author of many well-known Welsh hymns) was appointed curate of Amlwch in 1847, and showed a similar response to his surroundings. Although he was at Amlwch when his hymnal Y Psallwyr (a collection of 350 hymns based on the Psalms), was published in 1850, and it was also in Amlwch that he composed the poem Y Greadigaeth (The Creation), which won him the chair (albeit in somewhat controversial circumstances, with many of the audience disagreeing with the verdict of the adjudicators), the tone of his letters give the impression that he considered himself a lone litterateur without any literary circle in which to turn apart from the one he created for himself through corresponding with friends in Caernarfonshire.

Dafydd Ddu and Nicander were both outsiders who had come to Amlwch for a short time and then left, and had no regrets about leaving. They denounced the town and its people as being very philistine.

Amlwch did have its rough side, like any town of its kind which rose suddenly from a rush for minerals, where overcrowding , unemployment and poverty were major problems. Yet, it is easy to exaggerate, and in 1790, only a few years before Dafydd Ddu wrote a scathing description of the town, the Denbigh poet Twm o'r Nant published an anthology of his work called Gardd o Gerddi. This was done by collecting a list of people who had pledged in advance to buy a copy. Among the 700 or so subscribers were about 40 from Amlwch, including about half a dozen from Amlwch Port. These Amlwch subscribers include a doctor (Griffith Roberts MD), a schoolmaster (also called Griffith Roberts), various craftsmen, including a mason, a carpenter and a cartwright, a mechanic, an assayer, a tide surveyor and a gardener at Parys Lodge.

This list not only dispels the impression of Amlwch being totally devoid of culture, but also raises the question of who was Twm o'r Nant's contact in the area, to account for such a high representation among the subscribers. A possible candidate is the Rev David Ellis, who was a copier and collector of manuscripts, and who was a curate in Amlwch from 1782-88, and who pledged to buy three copies. A religious poem of his written in 1787, a translation of Ieuan Fardd's English poem The Penitent Shepherd, appears at the back of Gardd o Gerddi. At the front of the volume there is also a poem by Hugh Jones, mason, who is described as a poet in the list of subscribers. Clearly there was a good nucleus of literate people in the Amlwch area even at the very time when Dafydd Ddu was complaining of the lack of culture.

THOMAS JONES, TRANSLATOR

Thomas Jones (1777-1847) has largely been forgotten because his works did not furnish literary enjoyment, but his role in the culture of 19th century Wales is important since his books provided the means of learning to those who had learned to read in the Sunday schools.

The Sunday school movement was very effective in creating a cultural revolution in the island, by furnishing the ordinary people with an ability to red. In 1828 the Calvinistic Methodists alone had 94 Sunday schools in Anglesey, and a total of 11,000 pupils, and hundreds of people were learning to read. Thomas Jones's efforts both benefited from and promoted this process.

Thomas himself was the product of the Sunday school, and born in Llanfwrog in 1777, the son of a blacksmith.

In 1785 his father became a Methodist after hearing Michael Thomas, Llanddaniel, preaching at Llanrhuddlad chapel, and joined Caergeiliog chapel. He then arranged for preaching and a Sunday school to take place in his home in Llanfwrog, from which his own children and those of his neighbours.

Thomas had little more than a year of schooling in day schools, including those run by the parish sexton, by a Thomas Edwards of Llantrisant, and with the Rev John Evans, the Llanfwrog parish priest.

Yet he gained little from these. It was at his father's Sunday school, under his mother's tuition that he learned to read in English.

He started working at his father's forge, and then in various places including Amlwch, Caernarfon and Holywell. In around 1798 he joined Caergeiliog Calvinistic Methodist chapel, and in 1807 he started preaching.

By 1816 he lived at Pen 'rallt, a cottage near Bodedern, and started keeping a school at Bodedern for a short time before moving to keep a school at Amlwch until his death in July 1847. He became the master of the National School in Amlwch in 1822. As described already in the chapter about the National School, the school's financial situation was so poor that he had not been paid for months, and he asked the trustees for permission to levy a fee from his pupils. He also offered to train the singers for parish church services, and Gwalchmai refers to him teaching navigation to young ships' captains.

He continued to preach regularly during this time but was never ordained. It may be that he was too outspoken for the Methodists of his time. He considered getting emotional while preaching to be in poor taste and said so very clearly. He also disapproved of the idea of giving biblical, foreign names to chapels.

He also emphasised the importance of learning and the need for a college for training ministers, an area in which the Methodists were lagging behind the other denominations.

It was the same emphasis on knowledge which spurred his literary activity. He published eight books between 1824. He knew from experience that many had attended schools which were conducted in the medium of English without becoming proficient enough in that language to be ble to benefit from the instruction.

For this reason he wrote an arithmetic textbook in Welsh for Welsh people who were not sufficiently proficient in English, and then soon after prepared a geography textbook of 300pages, gathering information together well-known English works on the subject, and then translating them into Welsh. Afterwards he translated works by the American theologian Jonathan Edwards, namely A Treatise Concerning Religious Affection (1746), and A History of the Work of Redemption, and also The Christian Philosopher (1823) by the Scotsman Thomas Dick (1774-1857), a Bible commentary on the prophets by Thomas Scott (1742-1821), which ran to 675 pages, and a Bible concordance.

His aim was clearly to feed the cultural advances that came as a result of the Methodist awakening and the Sunday schools, by providing access to information that was previously not available in Welsh. These works amount to 2,600 pages, and while these works are of no great stylistic merit, and none of these are used as works of reference today, they do represent a heroic effort by a man of little formal education to use his spare hours to provide the materials for building a complete Christian culture.

REV WILLIAM ROBERTS

The Rev William Roberts (1784-1864) was a friend and contemporary of Thomas Jones, and became the leader of the Calvinistic Methodists in Anglesey after the death of John Elias. He was a capable denominational leader, and renowned as a great preacher, but his sermons are now lost to posterity, but some of his poetic works remain. These are not of the greatest poetic merit, but are typical of his time, in that putting theological truths into a metrical form took precedence over finesse in expression.

He became minister at Amlwch in 1817.

OTHER AUTHORS

By the time of William Roberts's death, a cultural tradition had developed in Amlwch. There were at least half a dozen Amlwch residents, who were of little significance in the eyes of the world, who wrote poetry. These included John M Edwards (Maelog Mon) and Owen Lewis (Philotechnicus 1800-86), Owen Edwards (Owain Eilian), John Lewis (Llew Elaeth, son of Philotechnicus), J Thomas (Morian), Hugh Hughes (Ieuan Glan Eilian, 1819-97), Evan Rowlands (Ynysog, 1842-99, who emigrated to California in 1863), and Thomas Roberts (Y Bardd Cloff, the lame bard). Although these poets were generally of no great merit, they do reflect a cultural change that had come to the town, and the fact that each had a bardic name indicates a society that respected culture, even if that culture was somewhat narrow and superficial.

The most interesting of these minor poets was Y Bardd Cloff. A pamphlet of his works was published in New York in 1864, which included two religious poems, a poem in memory of the Rev William Roberts, and a poem to the Sunday school. He was unable to use his hands and feet, but somehow taught himself to write with his mouth. A brother of his, called William, had emigrated to America and was a member of the Welsh Methodist Church in New York, where the minister was the Rev William

Roberts, Llannerchymedd. The minister arranged for the poems to be published and sold in America to help the disabled Amlwch poet.

From the above mentioned information it is clear that the growth of Nonconformity from 1780 onwards was a vital factor in the development of an interest in culture, and it seems that the high point of literature in Amlwch was from 1860-1900. The Sgolor Mawr complained that there was no bookshop in Amlwch when he was a teacher at the National School in 1854. Ten years later David Jones had opened a bookshop, and Hugh Hughes (Ieuan Glan Eilian) was also selling books at his drapers and grocery shop, and both boasted of selling a wide range of Welsh and English books.

In 1864 David Jones started printing books at 14 Wesley Street. At least 21 titles were printed between 1864 and 1891. As might be expected some of these dealt with religious topics, but there some on practical matters like a medical book by J C Roose (Chemicus, 1830-1913), a pharmacist who kept the Hibernian Drug Hall in Peter Street, and a Welsh version of Roger Mostyn's Ready Reckoner. The most numerous section of his publications was local history. Indeed in 1866, at about the same time as David Jones printed a book on the history of Amlwch by Thomas Pritchard (Rhen Graswr Elaeth), the other bookseller, Hugh Hughes countered this by a book on the same subject written by himself and printed on Lewis Jones's press in Llannerchymedd.

As well as books and booklets, David Jones also printed many leaflets of songs and poems, including some songs like Ceiriog's Bugeilio'r Gwenith Gwyn, many moral ballads, and ballads about murders and shipwrecks.

David Jones's press printed books by local authors, for a local audience which had acquired an ability to read in Welsh through the Sunday schools, but was unable to read much English. It may be no coincidence that one of the founders and the first editor of Anglesey's weekly newspaper Y Clorianydd, in 1891, John Hughes, Fron Deg (1858-1901), had been brought up in Amlwch during this time of a flourishing literary scene.

The one book from David Jones's press that is still valued for its contribution to knowledge is Methodistiaeth Mon by John Pritchard, published in 1888, which traces the development of Calvinistic Methodism in Anglesey from its beginnings in the 18th century, up to the 1880s. The author's thorough work in collecting and collating information on the denomination's history makes it a valuable work of reference.

John Pritchard was born in Tan y Bryn in 1821, and worked for a while at Parys Mountain, before spending some time at William Francis's school, and the at William Roberts's school in Holyhead. He then started preaching and went to the theological college at Bala. He returned to Amlwch in 1853 as minister of Penuel, Amlwch Port.

The one other book by an Amlwch author of significance is Mynydd Parys by Owen Griffith , Pen y Sarn, which was published in Caernarfon in 1897. Although it does not follow a logical plan, this book is interesting because of its reminiscences, and its descriptions of old characters is its real glory, sometimes rivalling Daniel Owen. Mynydd Parys deserves to be considered a minor classic .

THOMAS COWBURNE (1737?-1815), PRINTER

Among the Baron Hill papers at Bangor University there is a single printed sheet that exhorts volunteers to defend Great Britain against the threat from Napoleon, and the reference to the French taking Hanover allows us to date it soon after May 1803. This was printed by Thomas Cowburne, Amlwch.

He was clearly printing on a small scale in Amlwch, but 1812-14 he was in Bangor, and printed five books, none more than 16 pages each. On November 9, 1815 his obituary appeared in the North Wales Gazette says that he was a printer in Bangor, and formerly acting partner in the Amlwch Brewing Company.

The Amlwch parish register records the christening of five of his children between 1783 and 1795. In 1783 he is described as a grocer, but in 1786, 1788 and 1790 he is described as a brewer. No occupation is given in the 1795 entry.

The 1801 census shows him as being a shopkeeper living with his wife and six children at Llawr y Llan Isa. Llawr y Llan was also his address in the 1790s, as seen from the Land Tax Assessments of 1795-7.

An obituary in the Liverpool Mercury mentions Thomas Cowburne dying in Bangor at an advanced age in 1815, and mentions that he was formerly an eniment printer in Liverpool. He was a copper plate printer and bookseller in 1765-77, and printed a newspaper, the Liverpool Chronicle during 1767-68, though no copies of this paper seem to have survived, at least not in the British Library and in Liverpool city libraries.

He clearly moved from Liverpool to Amlwch sometime between 1777 and 1783, but the circumstances are uncertain. There was a brewery in Amlwch as early as 1784, in which the public were buying shares, clearly the Amlwch Brewing Company referred to in the obituary.

The fact that only a flyer from around 1803 is the only known example of his printing work at Amlwch suggests that his printing was a sideline, consisting of posters and other ephemeral works, while his shop and brewery were the real means of earning.

WILLIAM ROOS, ARTIST (1808-73

He was the grandson of Jonathan Roose (died February 6, 1813), who came to Amlwch in 1764 as foreman of the Roe mining company's works on Parys Mountain.

Jonathan settled at Mill Bank, Pentre'r Felin. His son was Thomas Roose, Bod-gadfa, Amlwch, and the son of Thomas and of his wife, Mary Parry of Holyhead, was William Roos the artist. By his birth in 1808 the family was settled in Anglesey.

Little is known of his early life, but a note on the back of his portrait of Mrs Ann Edwards of Caernarfon, dated 1859, suggests that William Roos had been a pupil of Mrs Edwards's father, namely William Francis, who kept a navigation school at Pen-bonc-llan, Amlwch.

There are suggestions that he spent some time learning in Italy, and that he went to an artist's studio in Dublin to have his portrait painted, specifically so that he could observe the artist's technique in mixing paint. The facts are remarkably few, but it would be fair to assume that he spent some time apprenticed to a portrait painter, and learned some techniques, though it is not known where, but this was certainly before 1835, as in that year he is mentioned as living in Caernarfon and was an artist, when he painted a portrait of the preacher Christmas Evans, who was a neighbour of his. This the first of Roos's portraits that is known.

He seems to have travelled a lot in the practice of his trade, as his obituary mentions him carrying on his business in London and Wrexham, and he seems to have some connection with the vicinity of Pennal, Merioneth, as his eldest son was born near Pennal in around 1849-50, and was buried there in 1872, a hint that perhaps his wife was from that area.

Sometime around 1877 Roos returned to Amlwch, and painted many portraits while there, but on returning from portraying one of the town's prominent people, he was struck with paralysis. He died on July 4, 1878, and was buried in Amlwch church cemetery.

He painted some dramatic historic scenes for Eisteddfod competitions, such as the death of Owain Glyndwr, and the death of Captain Wynn at the Battle of the Alma, for the Llangollen Eisteddfod in 1858, but also landscapes, watercolours and pastels, but it is for his portraits that he is most notable.

LOCAL CHARACTERS

CADI RONDOL

One of the colourful characters of Amlwch was Catherine Randal (1743-1828), commonly known as Cadi Rondol. It is likely that the Randals came to Amlwch with the first wave of incomers, during 1761-75, drawn by work at the Parys Copper Mines.

Catherine's mother, Jane Randal, lived at Parc Bach, near Glanrafon. And was buried in 1794. It seems that she had two daughters, since a wedding between Henry Watson and Ellen Randal took place on October 18, 1775, when Cadi was 32 years old. Interestingly, Ellen seems to have had enough education to be able to write her name, so it is likely that Cadi was also literate.

Cadi's story did not follow the same respectable vein as that of Ellen. She forgot her morals, and took up the world's oldest profession, and her swearing was proverbial. She was dangerous as John Jones, one of the deacons of Capel Mawr, discovered. When he tried to quieten her when she was cursing and swearing at everybody in the street, she turned, and threatened him with a knife.

But sometime after 1788 she was converted and became a regular attender at Capel Lletroed, and went from chapel to chapel to hear the gospel, and after having been prominent in the devil's service, she became notable as a godly woman.

Around 1800-1804 she was maid to the great Methodist preacher John Elias, and one day he rebuked her for singing a nursery rhyme to his son, rather than a hymn. Her response was: "Don't think, dear master, that I will sing a hymn to him. I won't give my Lord's praise to your child or anyone else."

BULL BAY

Now a small resort (called Porth Llechog in Welsh) but was once a pilot, fishing port and shipyard, and was once noted for fishing and smuggling, tow occupations which often appeared together. There is excellent sea bathing andthe so-called Roman Baths. The English name Bull Bay derives from a deep pool on the shore with the Welsh name Pwll y Tarw (the Bull's Pool).

Bull Bay had a lifeboat station from 1868-1926 and a pilot station in the day when shipping lines operated their own piloting services through a number of stations on the coast. Two four-oared sailing pilot boats were moored there. In the early 19th century Bull Bay, like many other bays along the Anglesey coast, had a small shipyard.

The first lifeboat station opened in 1868 and housed several lifeboats until 1904 when a new lifeboat house was built. The new lifeboat station was demolished in 1926 but the older building remains.

The coastline at this point was a favourite haunt of the Third Marquess of Anglesey, who intended to build another home here. In 1864 he commissioned Evan Pritchard to create a swimming bath which was completed, but the house was never built. The designer's flight of fancy created a medieval gateway flanked by round towers, complete with guard rooms. The entrance opened to a walled court with flower beds. There were stone dressing rooms from which a sloping pathway led down to the bath, cut out of the rock, 20 yards long by 10 feet wide. The 2 cleaned and refilled by each tide. Called the Roman Bath by local people, it has deteriorated since then. The building is now a ruin and only a cavity in the rock remains.

The Calvinistic Methodist cause at Bull Bay stated in 1893 as a Sunday school held in a dwelling , under the auspices of Bethesda chapel in Amlwch.

PORTH WEN BRICK WORKS

Slightly west of Bull Bay is the rather inaccessible bay of Porth wen once which housed a thriving brickworks. These brickworks were active from the end of the 19th century up to the First World War, producing high quality bricks of a yellow-white colour, which were valued for their quality of being able to withstand very high temperatures due to the high silica content in the clay, and therefore useful for the steel industry.

The date when the Porth Wen brickwork started is unknown, but a gravestone at the cemetery of St Eleth's church in Amlwch is for a man who died in an accident at Porth Wen brickworks in 1884.

By the early 20th century there was little employment in Amlwch due to the decline of the Parys mines, so workers would come from Amlwch to work there, despite the inaccessibility of the site. Three shifts were employed, as the kilns needed to be kept at a constant temperature day and night.

In 1906 a German called Steibel (the workers nicknamed him "Master Steeple") became the owner. He specialised in making bricks by the wire-cutting method. Two years later he was followed by Charles Tidy (who also managed the Cemaes brickworks), and remained in charge until the works closed in 1914. Tidy expanded the scope of the works, and introduced the press technique, producing glazed bricks and tiles.

The operation ceased in 1914. It seems that relations between the management and the workers were fraught, and errors in responding to changes in temperature resulted in batches of bricks being ruined.

The brickworks reopened in 1929, under the management of John Ready and the works struggled to survive through the 1930s and 1940s, but managed to survive after the Second World War. When it finally closed, all movable machinery was sold to a brickworks in Caernarfonshire. This was a difficult operation due to the steep terrain.

The site was not a very promising location for industry. Road transport was out of the question, as its location did not lend itself to making a road, and transport problems would have been a major factor in the closure of the works. There was a small quay, but the sea at Porth Wen often carried a heavy swell, and ship owners would be loth to let their ships stay at the quayside when they were likely to be damaged by striking the rocky sea bed, so that insurers were reluctant to underwrite suvh a risk.

Nowadays the site can be visited by a half mile walk, on a narrow path from the road, where a battery of beehive shaped kilns, tall chimney stacks and the deserted quay remain to remind the visitor of the site's industrial past.

LLANEILIAN

This small village to the east of Amlwch Port is dominated by the lighthouse of Point Lynas, which overlooks the cove of Porth Eilian, and has an ancient church dedicated to Saint Eilian, which is of great interest.

The church has a stocky square tower crowned with a simple stone spire in a pyramidal shape, which was built about 800 years ago. The chancel and the nave were rebuilt in the 15th century.

Illustration 8: The Church of St Eilian

The church stands above the tiny bay of Porth yr Ychain (Port of the Oxen), which according to tradition was where St Eilian landed with his family and possessions in the 6th century . The saint is said to have restored the sight of Prince Caswallon who in thanks, gave him land on which to settle.

The reputed site of Caswallon's palace, Llys Caswallon is on Mynydd Eilian, nearby, a mile south south east of Llaneilian church, though there is a modern house of the same name on the opposite side of the road to the old site.

Eilian's well, Ffynnon Eilian, on the coast half a mile north west of Llaneilian church, and now in ruins, was reputed for its curative powers. Eilian built his cell near to his landing place, and the present chapel attached to the church is said to have been on the site of his shrine, which was a place of worship in the 6th century. There is also a tongs used for separating fighting dogs in the 18th century, at a time when church services were less sedate than today.

The church contains an ancient portrait of Saint Eilian, and the rood screen carries a painting of a skeleton as the grim reaper, with the inscription "Colyn Angau yw Pechod" (Sin is the sting of death"), which emphasises mortality. Wood carvings include angels playing musical instruments.

Illustration 9: The rood loft at Llaneilian church

Illustration 10: The Grim Reaper painting on the rood loft

The old oil painting of Saint Eilian shows him as having five fingers and a thumb. This may be an error on the part of the artist, or may be derived from a tradition that the saint had this deformity.

The chapel of Saint Eilian, at an angle to the chancel, and connected to it by a 17th century passage, dates from the late 14th or early 15th century. This small chapel was the focus of quasi pagan celebrations on the saint's day. People would attempt to lie in Eilian's chest, a church chest measuring four foot square by three feet deep. Anyone who could turn round in the confined space would have his or her life extended for another year, or so it was believed. A narrow division in a wooden panel in the church presented a challenge to young people to pass through it without touching the sides, for good luck. But failure reversed the good fortune. These were times when superstition was rife, and it took the Roundheads, and later the Nonconformists especially, to stamp out these superstitious practices.

William Bulkeley commented in his diary on July 27, 1740 that the congregation at Llanfechell was small due to a superstitious pilgrimage to Llaneilian to "visit a dry skull... and playing other Jugling tricks".

As the port of Liverpool expanded, it was felt by 1766 that there was a need for a pilot station on Anglesey from where ships could pick up a pilot to take them safely in and out of the Mersey. Before that time, pilotage was privately operated with no supervision.

In 1764, 18 ships had been stranded and more than 75 lives lost. Traffic in and out of the Mersey was increasing rapidly. In 1766 the first Liverpool Pilotage Act was passed, which allowed for pilots to be based at Point Lynas.

Ships approaching Point Lynas had to hoist their colours and show lights or fire guns by night and run close inshore so they could be boarded in still water.

By 1896 steam had taken over and two ships were based at Point Lynas. Forty-three pilots were attached, including two masters. Thirteen pilots remained ashore for harbour duty. Later motor vessels were used.

At first the early pilots used a farmhouse as their lookout post. From 1779 they used two oil lamps with small metal reflectors set into a tower and showing in two directions, and there was a flagstaff for day signals. The first lighthouse at Point Lynas was built in 1791, and the present lighthouse was built in 1835 by the Mersey Docks and Harbour Board at a cost of £1,165. The lighthouse is a low castellated building painted white with round lens rooms connected to the seaward side of the house.

Trinity House assumed responsibility for the Point Lynas lighthouse in 1973. It was electrified in 1951 and automated in 1989. There is an automatic fog detector which activates the fog signal should visibility drop to less than two and a half miles. The old pilot house no longer exists.

Robert Beaver was at one time responsible for the lighthouse and pilot station on a voluntary basis, although he did benefit from the occasional cask of wine which might have slipped the notice of customs at Holyhead, and he had useful deliveries of coal and cloth. He took over responsibility for the Point Lynas lighthouse in 1782, after ill-health forced him a colourful life at sea as a trader and the captain of a Liverpool privateer. He died in 1814 aged 65.

The telecommunications masts on Mynydd Eilian are a reminder of the earlier method of sending messages, when a semaphore station stood on the high land above Point Lynas. This was the third station in the line running from South Stack, near Holyhead, signalling messages to a similar station on Puffin Island, to be relayed several more times along the coast before arriving at Liverpool.

In 1841 the semaphore station was replaced by a telegraph station. Although the semaphore system has been so efficient that a message from Holyhead to Liverpool could be received in less than a minute, electrical transmission was taking over throughout the country.

USEFUL WEBSITES

The following websites can be useful:

The Copper Kingdom http://www.copperkingdom.co.uk/ This is the siteof the Amlwch Industrial Heritage Trust, with its museum and sites relating to the copper industry.

Amlwch Data: http://www.amlwchdata.co.uk/ A rich resource for historical information, archive photographs, and genealogical resources.

Anglesey County Council: http://www.anglesey.gov.uk/ General website for the Anglesey County Council.

Printed in Great Britain
by Amazon

87217969R00029